Teacher's Book.

HERE COMES SUPER BUS 3
Activity Book

María José Lobo ◆ Pepita Subirà

CONTENTS

Name ....

School .... Class ....

INTRODUCTION

1 ◆ Read, find and write   What are the children's names?

1. Rory   2. ....   3. ....   4. ....   5. ....   6. ....

Hi! I'm Charles. I've got fair hair. I'm wearing a tracksuit and white trainers.

Hello! My name's Sophie. I've got long brown hair. I'm wearing glasses.

Hello! I'm Rachel. I'm wearing a skirt, a blouse and black shoes.

Hi! My name's Rory. I'm very tall. I'm wearing jeans and a jumper.

Hello! My name's Sue. I've got fair hair. I'm wearing trousers and a cap.

Hi! My name's Peter. I'm wearing trousers, a jumper and black shoes.

2 ◆ Guessing game   Write and guess.

Example ...... *She has got long black hair. She is wearing* ....
a skirt, a blouse and black shoes. Who is she? ....

....

....

....

....

3 **Match and write**

1d sand
....
....
....
....
....
....
....

4 **Read and write** What is the title?

family   ~~parts of the body~~   the house   animals

parts of the body ....

head	*kitchen*	*lion*	*mum*
ears	*living room*		

INTRODUCTION

5 Read and circle Odd man out.

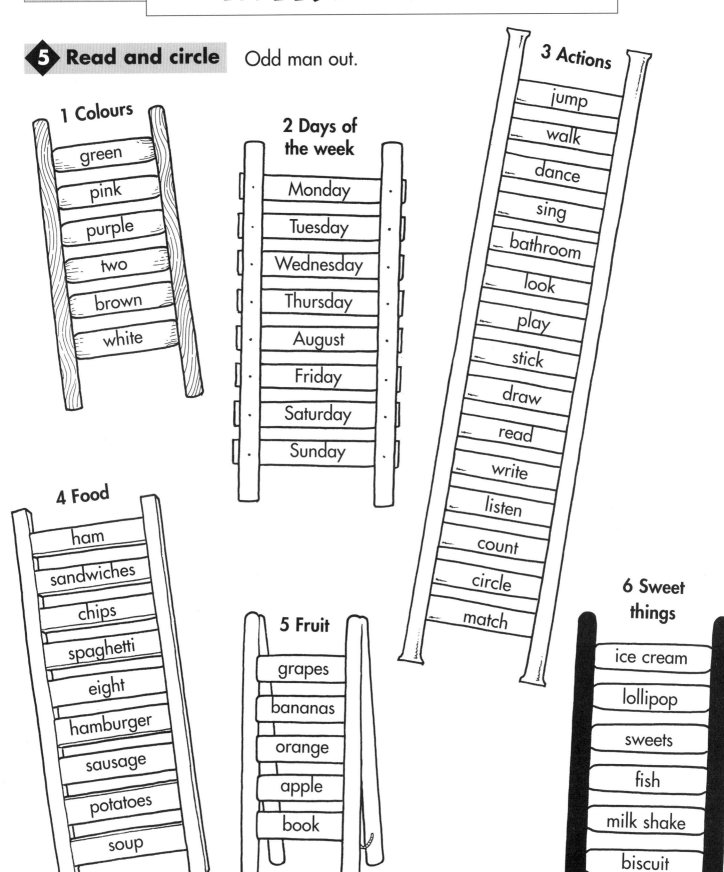

1 Colours

green
pink
purple
two
brown
white

2 Days of the week

Monday
Tuesday
Wednesday
Thursday
August
Friday
Saturday
Sunday

3 Actions

jump
walk
dance
sing
bathroom
look
play
stick
draw
read
write
listen
count
circle
match

4 Food

ham
sandwiches
chips
spaghetti
eight
hamburger
sausage
potatoes
soup

5 Fruit

grapes
bananas
orange
apple
book

6 Sweet things

ice cream
lollipop
sweets
fish
milk shake
biscuit
cake

INTRODUCTION

6 Circle and say Find the safe bridges.

1. a b c d e f g h i j k l m n o p q r s t u v w x y z

2. a b c d e f g h i j k l m n o p q r s t u v w x y z

3. a b c d e f g h i j k l m n o p q r s t u v w y x z

4. a b c d e f g h i j k l m n o p q r s t u v w x y z

7 Solve Can you make 15 numbers?

1 7 2

1 2 7 12 17 21 27 71 72 127 172 217 271 712 721

1 5 8

1 5 8 15

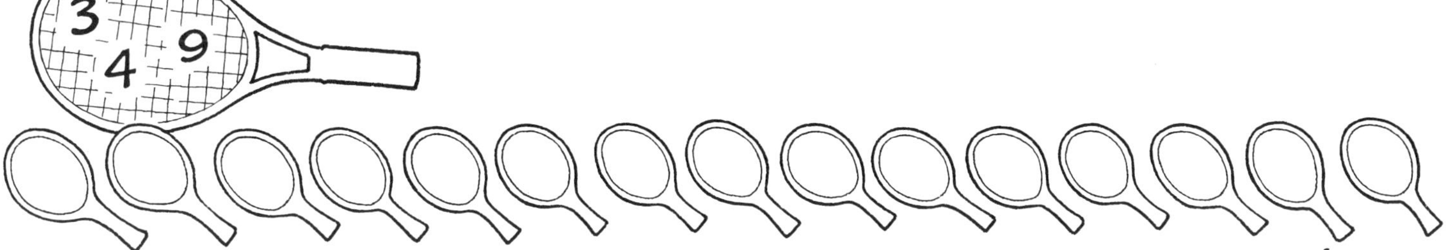

3 4 9

five ◆ 5

1 POEMS AND CONTESTS

1 Crossword   Write the names of the school subjects.

Down ↓   Across ⇒

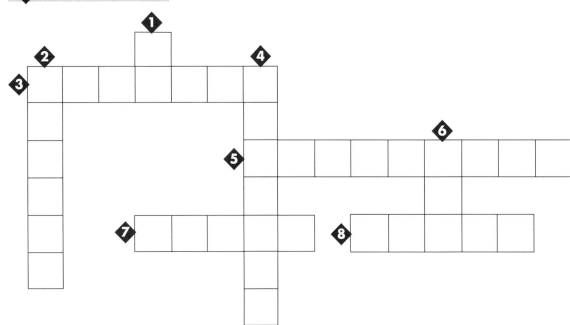

2 Draw and write   What time is it?

It's ten to six.

It's twenty past nine.

It's eleven o'clock.

It's twenty-five to twelve.

1 It's ....

....

3 It's ....

....

2 It's ....

....

4 It's ....

....

6 ◆ six

3 Circle and write Spot five mistakes.

In the story James is studying a poem for a (radio) contest. The poem is very easy. The contest is on Monday. James says the poem to grandpa in the living room and in the kitchen. In the contest, James gets 20 points. He is the winner.

In the story James is studying a poem for a TV contest.

....

....

....

....

....

....

4 Write and say

Music is magic

You hear it in your ears

It is in the sand

It is in the wind

And it makes you sing

Music is magic

You feel it in your body

And it makes you dance

5 Write your poem

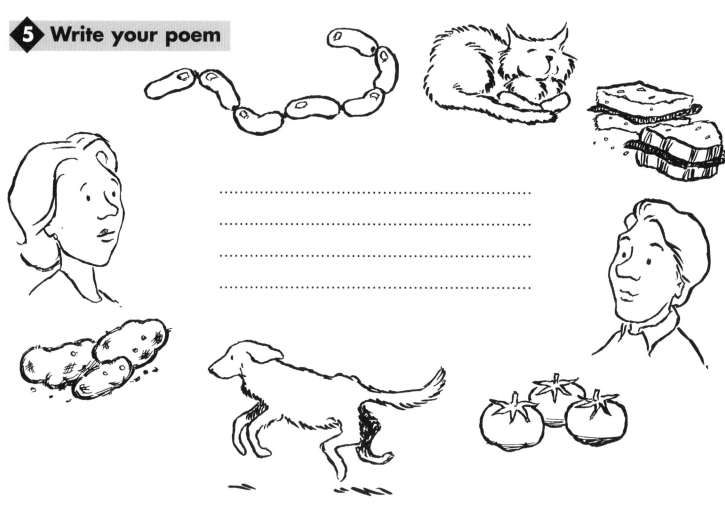

....

....

....

....

6 Read and tick (✓) True or false?

Look at the timetable on Pupil's Book page 10.

	True	False
1 English classes are on Mondays, Tuesdays, Wednesdays and Fridays.	✓	
2 School lunch is at two o'clock.		
3 Maths is on Wednesdays at ten past eleven.		
4 Classes begin at ten o'clock.		
5 The break finishes at twenty past eleven.		

7 Listen and write the subjects 📼

	Monday	Tuesday	Wednesday	Thursday	Friday
9.00 - 9.45	History	P.E.	English		History
9.45 - 10.30	French		History	Music	
10.30 - 10.55	← B R E A K →				
10.55 - 11.45	Maths		Maths	Maths	Drama
11.45 - 12.30	Geography		Drama	Geography	French
12.30 - 1.45	← L U N C H →				
1.45 - 2.30	Swimming	Art	Science	Sports	Art
2.30 - 3.15					Science

8 Read and write

1 What's your favourite subject?..

2 What's your favourite school day?..

3 What subject have you got on Tuesdays at nine?..

4 What subjects have you got on Wednesday mornings?...

5 What subjects have you got on Friday afternoons?..

◆9 Look, count and write

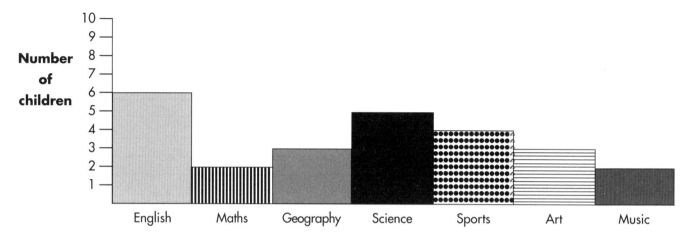

Favourite subjects

Favourite subjects	Number of children
English	6
....	....
....	....
....	....
....	....
....	....
....	....

◆10 Read and match

act out   cut out

sing a song

play a game

say a chant

draw and colour

write   listen

DO YOU KNOW THAT...?

Look at Pupil's Book page 12.

1 ▶ Find and write

1 Nursery rhymes are old .... for little children.

2 Many poems are 'action rhymes'. This means that you do an .... when you say the poem.

3 Some .... are in shapes.

4 There are 65 .... in the world.
This is some of the Roman ....
This is some of the Greek ....
This is some of the Arabic ....

2 ▶ Write and say

warm

close

My house is .... and

big

and

the door.

Come in

....

 Test yourself How many words can you write?

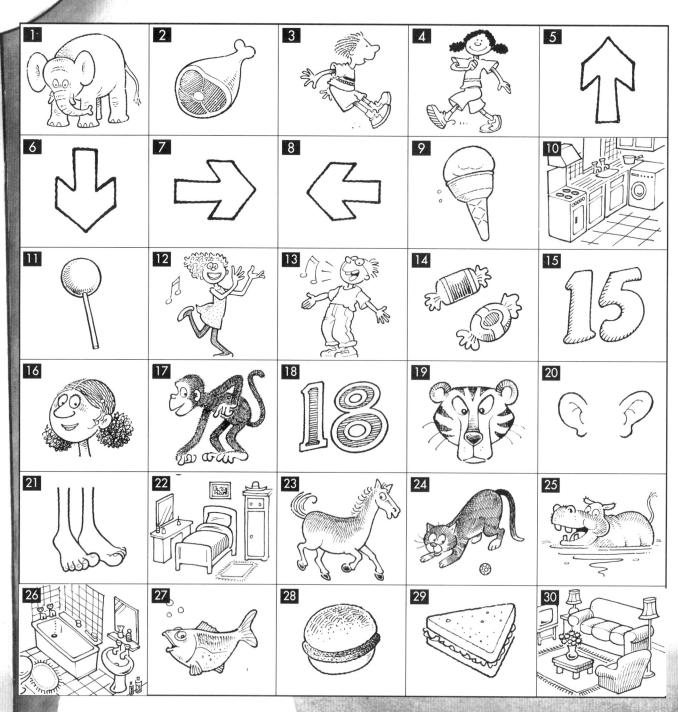

SUPER BUS STOP 1

1 *elephant*	11	21
2	12	22
3	13	23
4	14	24
5	15	25
6	16	26
7	17	27
8	18	28
9	19	29
10	20	30

SCORE

1–10	Not very good. Study more.	21–26	Very good.
11–15	Okay, but you can do better.	27–30	Excellent. Well done!
16–20	Good.		

2 Look and write What class is this?

1 *History*

2

3

4

5

6

1 Read and match

1st 2nd 3rd 4th 5th ....

sixth   seventh   eighth

first   fourth   twelfth   ninth

second

third   fifth   eleventh   tenth

2 Listen, number and match

switch off the computer   switch on the computer

type your name   click on the mouse

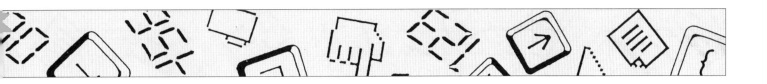

3 Tick (✓) True or false?

		True	False
1	The children are playing Geography games.	....	....✓....
2	The new computer is laughing.	....	....
3	The computer is very fast.	....	....
4	The computer has got the 'Eating Virus'.	....	....
5	The virus disappears at the end of the story.	....	....

4 Classify, speak and write

Months

....

....

....

....

Pets

....

....

....

....

Ordinal Numbers

....

....

....

....

Fruit

....

....

....

....

Collections

....

....

....

....

August	*third*
banana	*parrot*
fifth	*grapes*
dog	*stamps*
coins	*rabbit*
orange	*January*
March	*lemon*
stickers	*eighth*
ninth	*hamster*
December	*postcards*

5 Listen, circle and write

Steven   Clare   John   Karen

March
1 2 3 4 5 6
7 8 9 10 11 12 13
14 15 16 17 18 19 20
21 22 23 24 25 26 27
28 29 30 31

August
1 2 3 4 5 6 7
8 9 10 11 12 13 14
15 16 17 18 19 20 21
22 23 24 25 26 27 28
29 30 31

February
1 2 3 4
5 6 7 8 9 10 11
12 13 14 15 16 17 18
19 20 21 22 23 24 25
26 27 28

Karen's birthday is on the .... of ....

Clare's birthday is ....

Steven's birthday is ....

John's birthday is ....

6 Read, find out and tick (✓)   Look at the story pages in your Pupil's Book and tick the pictures where:

Pictures	1	2	3	4	5	6	7	8	9
The children are working in groups	✓								
John is clicking on the mouse		✓							
Karen and John are playing the 222 Game		✓	✓	✓	✓				
The computer is laughing		✓	✓	✓	✓	✓	✓		
Karen is pressing the return key								✓	
The computer is saying 'Do you want to play the 222 Game again?'									✓

TB p 48

TB p 48

7 Look and write

talk ~~talk~~ draw
laugh write
listen play

They
1 A boy and a girl are talking

2 ....

3 ....

4 ....

5 ....

6 ....

8 Puzzle   Find and speak. What are they playing?

cards
computer game
dominoes
chess

Example: Clare's playing cards.

→Dominoes TB p49

→Dominoes TB p49

seventeen ◆ 17

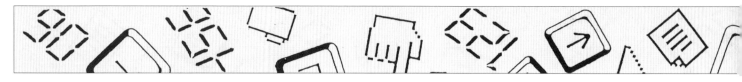

9 Computer maze TB p50

Solve the riddles and follow the road with the correct answer.

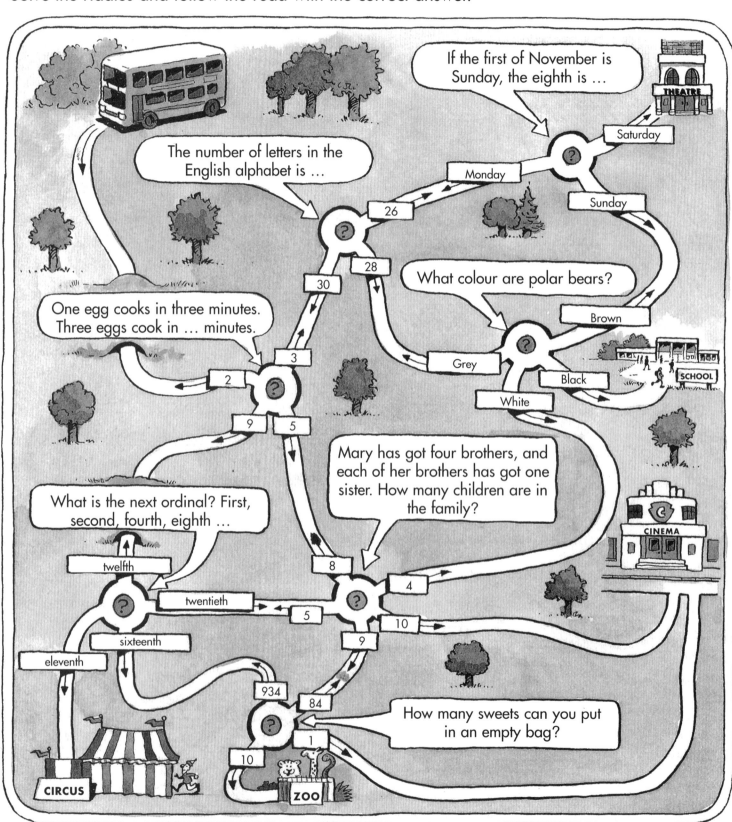

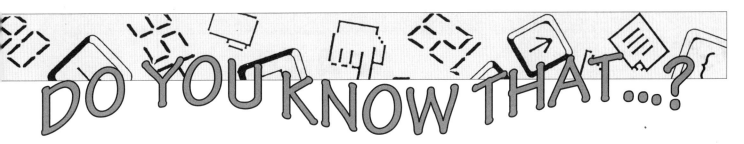

DO YOU KNOW THAT...?

Look at Pupil's Book page 18.

Look at Pupil's Book page 18.

1 Number

1 **Old Computers**

4 **Dog Robots**

2 **MODERN COMPUTERS**

5 **Internet**

3 **What's a Virus?**

2 Read, match and complete

1 ..C. Look, this is the first computer. It is .....30............ metres long.

2 ..b... Portable computers are very ....Small...... .

3 ..a... Surfing the ....Internet..... is good fun!

4 ..d... A virus can destroy your ....Computer

5 ..e... Robots can imitate human and ....animal.... actions.

a

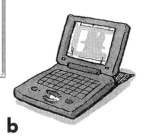

b

c

d

e

1 Puzzle Find, write and draw.

Find four objects you can see in the sky.
Join the letters of the same type.

moon

Sun

comet

Star

2 Read and match

1 There are lots of bright ....Stars...... in the sky.

2 The name of our planet is ...Earth....... .

3 The ...Sun........ is a star.

4 At night we can see the ....Moon..... .

5 ..Comets... have got a big head and a long tail.

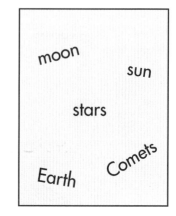

moon

sun

stars

Earth   Comets

Listen, circle and write 🔊 Circle the objects mentioned in the story.

comet

the Sun

anorak

camera ✓

books

binoculars ✓

planet

slippers ✓

comet ✓

roller skates

stars ✓

torch ✓

boots

the Moon

4 **Memory game**

Look at the first picture in the story.
Read and answer the questions:

1 What day is it? ....It's Saturday........

2 What are they doing? ....They are having breakfast..........

3 Who is reading the newspaper? ..Mum is reading the newspaper.

4 Who wants to see the comet? ..Julie wants to see the comet.

5 Read, match and write

a

> This is a picture of me and my school friends swimming in the pool. We've got swimming lessons on Tuesdays at eleven.

1 b

b

> On Saturdays we have a big breakfast. My brother Andrew isn't in the picture. He's sleeping. He's one year old.

2 c

c

> This is a picture of me, my brother Martin and my two cousins. Their names are Brenda and Emma. Brenda is twelve and Emma is seven. On Sundays they come to my house and we play football in the garden.

3 a

Write about one picture. Picture number ☐

What day is it?...

What time is it?...

What are they doing?...

6 Speak and tick (✓) Ask five friends. Can you …?

Name	canoe	skate	swim	ride a bike	ski jump	ride a horse	play floor hockey

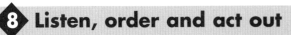

7 Pairs game   Speak, do and write.

Can you wink? _Yes, I can._

Can you whistle? _No, I can't_

Can you sing a song in English? _Yes, I can_

Can you count from 10 to 100 in tens? _Yes, I can_

Can you hop ten times on your left leg? _Yes, I can._

Can you touch your left ear with your right hand? _Yes, I can_

Can you move your ears? ....

Can you spell your name? ....

Can you mime 'I don't know'? ....

8 Listen, order and act out   Write the dialogue in the correct order and act it out.

Tr 33

Are you OK, love?

Look! The comet's over there!

Look! It's over there!

Mum   Julie

Oh, yes! There it is! I can see it now. Look, look! Look! Ow!

Where? I can't see it!

Yes, I can see the comet and lots of stars!

Look! The comet's over there!

Where? I can't see it

Look! It's over there

Oh yes! There it is I can see it now. Look, look, look, Ow!

Are you ok, love?

Yes, I can see the comet and lots of stars

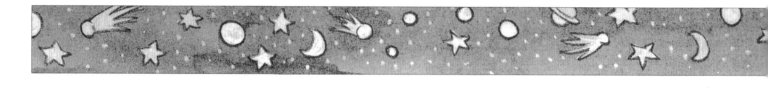

9 Read and tick (✓)   What do the newspapers say?

the News	THE SUN	the Comet
Halley's comet. This evening at eight o'clock. Only once every 76 years. Don't miss it!	Take your binoculars and go to Mossy Hill. Halley's comet visits us again.	After 76 years, Halley's Comet arrives again. See it from Mossy Hill today at 8PM.

Do the newspapers say these things?	the News	the Sun	the Comet
The name of the comet	✓	✓	✓
How often you can see it	✓	—	✓
The time you can see it	✓	—	✓
Where you can see it	—	✓	✓
What to take with you	—	✓	—

10 Write about Halley's comet

theStar ★

May 11 .... 200.17...

Halley's comet! This evening at nine o'clock at the Rheinbridge. Take your binoculars, popcorn and fireworks. Once every ten years. Don't miss it!

DO YOU KNOW THAT...?

Look at Pupil's Book page 26.

1 Can you read these words?   Write the words out as in the example.

Galaxy
Galaxy

YAW YXJIM (MILKY WAY)
Milky Way

HALLEY
Halley

THEMOON
the Moon

2 Read and tick (✓)   True or false?

		True	False
1	There are twenty-five stars in the Milky Way.		✓
2	All stars are round.	✓	
3	All stars are yellow.		✓
4	The Sun is an old star.		✓
5	There are footprints of astronauts on the Moon.	✓	
6	Mars is a very important star. *planet*		✓
7	Halley's comet is very big.	✓	

3 Solve

Halley's comet will appear again in 2062 and +76 = 2138 .

1 **Test yourself**   How many words can you write?

Can you … ?

1 *swim*
2 *skip*
3 *dive*
4 *climb*
5 *skate*
6 *ski*
7 *drive*
8 *wink*

9 *whistle*
10 *ride a horse*
11 *fly*
12 *cycle*
13 *hop*
14 *play tennis*
15 *jump*

SCORE

1–5	Not very good. Study more.
6–8	Okay, but you can do better.

9–11	Good.
12–13	Very good.
14–15	Excellent. Well done!

2 Write

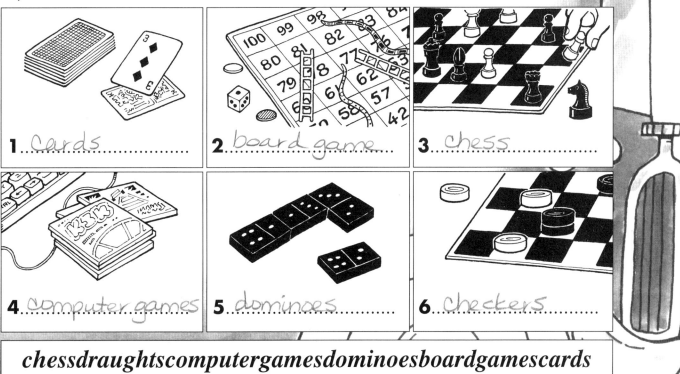

1 *Cards*
2 *board game*
3 *chess*
4 *computer games*
5 *dominoes*
6 *checkers*

chessdraughtscomputergamesdominoesboardgamescards

1 Match and write Where are they?

*under the table
next to the sofa
behind the tree
~~in front of the shelf~~
on the fridge
between his mum and dad
in the wardrobe*

Grandma is ....

The wolf is ....

Superduck is *in front of the shelf.*

Blacky is ....

Pretty Ritty is ....

Jerry is ....

Jimmy Ghost is ....

2 **Read and write**   What is Brainy saying?

Switch off the computer!
They're under the chair!
It's next to the computer!
They're on top of your head!
Switch off the light!

1

Where's my bag?

Woof! Woof!
....
....

2

Oh, it's next to the computer.
Now, where are my glasses?

Woof! Woof!
....
....

3

Woof! Woof!
....

OK, OK, Brainy!
The computer's on.

4

Woof! Woof!
....

OK, Brainy.
The light's on.
Now it's off.

5

Where are my keys?

Woof! Woof!
....
....

3 Pairs game   Draw four objects and ask questions.

Child A

Where's ...?

Where are ...?

Child B

Where's ...?

Where are ...?

4 Crossword

1 It has got two wheels. You ride it.

2 It is very long and it has got a lot of wheels.

3 It can fly but it hasn't got wings.

4 It has got two wings and it flies.

5 It has got four wheels. Its name begins with a C.

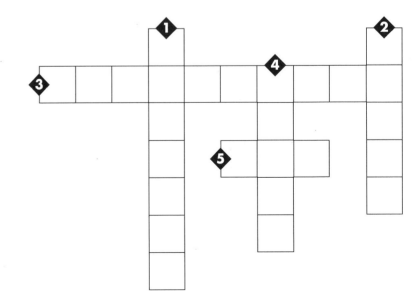

5 Listen, draw and write 🎧 Tr 40 TB p 77

Draw each route in a different colour.

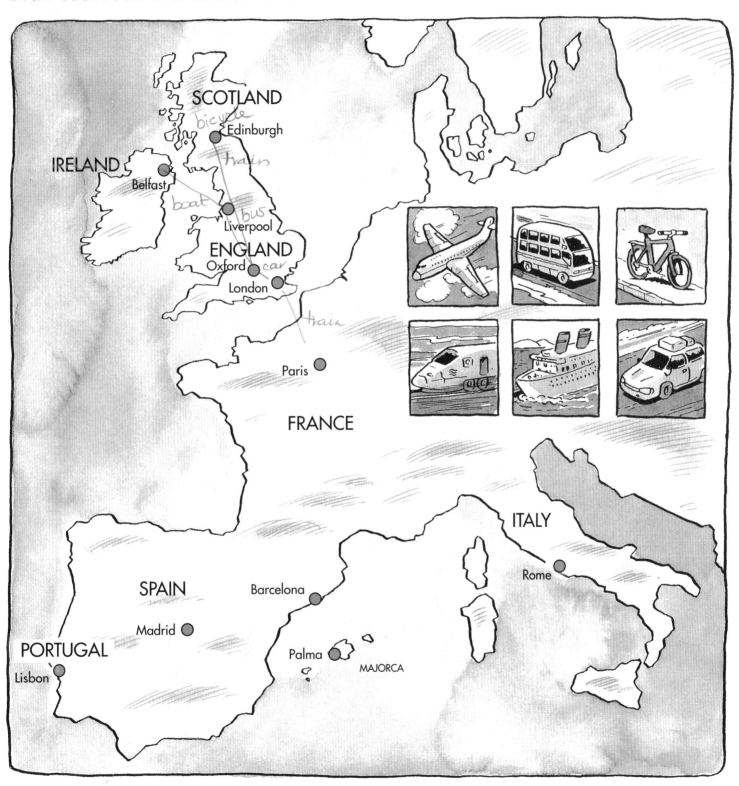

6 **Speak and write** Ask three friends and write *Yes* or *No*.

Ask 'Yes I do' 'No I don't'

	me			
Do you have breakfast at home?				
Do you make your bed?				
Do you go to school by bus?				
Do you go to school by car?				
Do you clean your shoes?				
Do you have lunch at home?				

7 **Listen, draw the times and write** Steve's ideal day.

1

Steve gets up at ten o'clock

2

He has breakfast at half past ten.

3

He plays basketball at a quarter past ele[v]

4

He has lunch at one o'clock

5

He goes to the cinema by bus at four o'clock

6

He has dinner at seven o'clock

7

He watches TV at half past nine.

8

He goes to bed at twelve.

plays basketball
has dinner
goes to bed
goes to the cinema by bus
~~gets up~~
has lunch
watches TV
has breakfast

8 **Write** Now write about your ideal day.

DO YOU KNOW THAT...?

Look at Pupil's Book page 32.

1 Find and write   What's the name?

1 A famous train _Orient Express_

2 A fast plane _Concorde_

3 A train that goes under the sea _Le Shuttle_

4 A fast Spanish train _AVE_

2 Read and tick (✓)   True or false?

	True	False	I don't know
1 The Orient Express is a plane.		✓	
2 Concorde is a plane.	✓		
3 You can go from London to New York in three hours.	✓		
4 The AVE goes from Madrid to Seville in two and a half hours.	✓		
5 You can go from London to Venice in five days.			✓
6 Helicopters are fast planes.		✓	

1 Listen and write

CD 2 Tr 1

 Susan

 Bill

 Rachel

Where are you going?
I'm going to Mossy Hill. ....

How are you going?
I'm going by bicycle. ....

2 Match, read and write — Who are they? Where are they going?

CD 2 Tr 2

  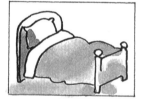  

Little Red Riding Hood ....

I'm going to my grandma's house

~~Little Red Riding Hood is going to her grandma's house.~~

Super Bus is going to school.   Jerry is going to bed.

Superduck is going to the supermarket.

Mr Magico is going to the circus.

3 Read, listen and tick (✓) True or false?

	True	False
1 The children are going to Lonely House.	✓	
2 They are going on their bicycles.		
3 Jane is a new girl in the group.		
4 Victor likes Jane.		
5 There is a cat in Lonely House.		
6 There is a big storm.		
7 Jane is afraid.		
8 The other children are afraid.		

4 Write your own chant

1

In an old, old town
there is an old, old street
and in the old, old street
there is an old, old shop
and in the old, old shop
there is a LOLLIPOP!

My Chant

....

....

....

....

....

....

....

....

2

In a big, big river
there is a big, big cave
and in the big, big cave
there is ... a CROCODILE!

5 Complete the graph   Are you afraid of …?

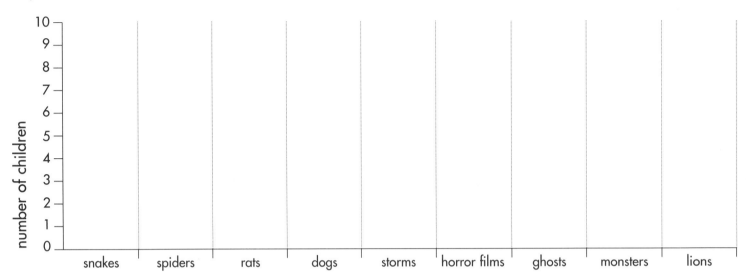

I'm afraid of ……………………………………………………………………………………………

I'm not afraid of ……………………………………………………………………………………

6 Listen and match   Where are they? What's the weather like?

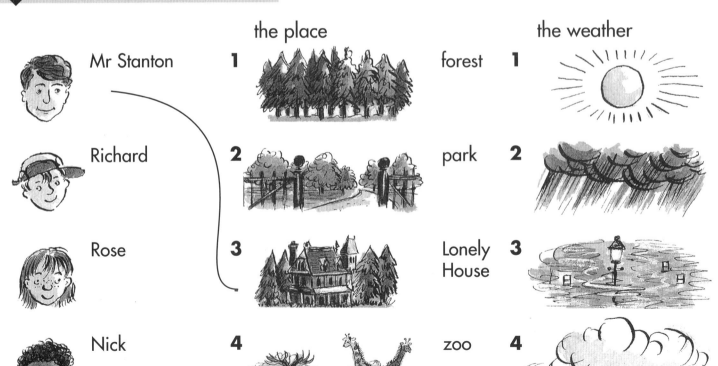

Mr Stanton	the place		the weather
Mr Stanton	1	forest	1
Richard	2	park	2
Rose	3	Lonely House	3
Nick	4	zoo	4

7 Read and circle

Emma loves excursions. She's going on an excursion on Saturday the 7th. This is her diary.

FRIDAY 6

1
2
3
4

Tomorrow is a special day. I'm going to the Lake District with my sports club. We are going there by bus. The bus leaves at 7 a.m., so I must get up at 6 a.m.!
I need:
my boots
thick socks
my anorak
my tracksuit
my gloves
I can't wait!

5
6
7
8
9
10
11
12

SATURDAY 7

Here we are! The Lake District is fantastic ... on sunny days! But today it's raining a lot! I'm writing this diary in the youth hostel. From the window I can see lots of trees and flowers. There is a very old house at the top of a hill and a small lake near the house. We're going to the lake this afternoon for a picnic... in the rain!

1
2
3
4
5
6
7
8
9
10
11

8 Choose your own adventure   You are going on an excursion.

Tick (✓) one box in each section.

Where are you going?

I'm going …   ☐ to a cave   ☐ to the forest   ☐ to the beach

☐ to a lake   ☐ ....

How are you going?

I'm going …   ☐ by bus   ☐ on foot   ☐ by bicycle

☐ by train   ☐ ....

Who's going with you?

I'm going with …   ☐ my friends   ☐ my family   ☐ my brother

☐ my dog   ☐ ....

But …   ☐ I see a snake   ☐ there is a storm

☐ I see a strange house   ☐ I see an old woman

And I ....

Write your complete adventure here:

....

....

....

....

....

DO YOU KNOW THAT...?

Look at Pupil's Book page 38.

❶ .Count the words and complete

1 'Storm' appears ....*3*.... times in the text.

2 'Thunder' appears .... times in the text.

3 'Lightning' appears .... times in the text.

4 'Hurricane' appears .... times in the text.

5 'Rain' appears .... times in the text.

6 'Wind' appears .... times in the text.

❷ Read and tick (✓) True or false?

	True	False
1 'Storm' means 'good weather'.	....	✓
2 Rain, wind and thunder are normally part of a storm.	....	....
3 Light travels faster than sound.	....	....
4 A typhoon is a hurricane.	....	....
5 Tornadoes are not destructive.	....	....

❸ Solve

Lisa hears the thunder 5 seconds after she sees the lightning. How far away is the storm?

....

SUPER BUS STOP 3

1 Test yourself How many words can you write?

1 *car* .... **8** .... **15** ....

2 .... **9** .... **16** ....

3 .... **10** .... **17** ....

4 .... **11** .... **18** ....

5 .... **12** .... **19** ....

6 .... **13** .... **20** ....

7 .... **14** ....

SCORE

1–6	Not very good. Study more.	11–13	Good.
7–10	Okay, but you can do better.	14–17	Very good.
		18–20	Excellent. Well done!

◆ 2 Match and write   What do you do at …?

1 *I have breakfast at a quarter past eight*

2 ....

3 ....

4 ....

5 ....

6 ....

have lunch   do homework   ~~have breakfast~~   go to bed   go to school   watch TV

6 MY NEIGHBOURHOOD

1 Write What is there in your neighbourhood?

My neighbourhood

....

There is a ....

....

....

....

There are some ....

....

....

....

There aren't any ....

....

....

....

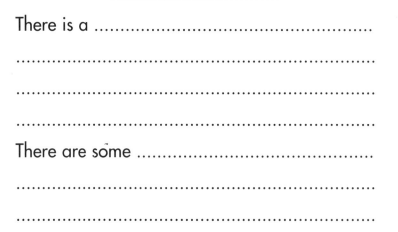

2 Listen, look and answer At the beginning of the story …

1 Is it dark or light on Dustbin planet?

a dark   **b** light

2 Is the smell horrible or nice?

a horrible   **b** nice

3 Are the streets clean or dirty?

a clean   **b** dirty

4 Are the trees dead or alive?

a dead   **b** alive

5 Are the buildings high or low?

a high   **b** low

6 Are the people happy or sad?

a happy   **b** sad

3 Read and complete

trees   rubbish   horrible   rivers   pollution   masks

This is Dustbin Planet. The .... here is very bad. There is a
lot of .... on the ground and the smell is ....
People live in skyscrapers and they wear oxygen ....
The Sun doesn't shine on Dustbin Planet. It's dark. There aren't any ....
There aren't any flowers. Everything is dead.
The .... are dirty. The seas are dirty. There is rubbish everywhere:
plastic bags, paper, bottles, tins and cans.

forty-five ◆ 45

4 Circle and speak

Don't cycle in the street.
Cycle in the cycle path.

litter bin

5 Read and tick (✓)   How green are you?

		Yes	No
1	Do you know this sign? ♻	☐	☐
2	Do you come to school by car?	☐	☐
3	Do you plant flowers?	☐	☐
4	Do you throw crisp packets on the ground?	☐	☐
5	Do you use recycled paper?	☐	☐
6	Do you use the litter bins in the park?	☐	☐
7	Do you pick wild flowers?	☐	☐
8	Do you know the colour of the recycling bins?	☐	☐
9	Do you remember to switch off lights?	☐	☐
10	Do you climb trees?	☐	☐

You score 1 point for each **YES** answer to questions 1, 3, 5, 6, 8 and 9, and 1 point for each **NO** answer to questions 2, 4, 7 and 10.

If you score:
- 9–10 points: Well done! Excellent!
- 5–8 points: Not bad! You can do better.
- 0–4 points: Awful! You're not green.

6 Read and write   True or false?

7th April 2000

3, Park Rd.
Jameston
Rutland
RU11 0YE
Great Britain

Dear Pen-friend,
My name's Ruth. I live with my parents and my brother Jeff in Jameston. Jameston is a small green village near Nottingham. The village is beautiful and clean. There aren't any high buildings in Jameston.
My house isn't very big. Downstairs there is a hall, a dining room, a kitchen and a toilet.
Upstairs there is a bathroom and three bedrooms. One for my parents, one for my brother and one for me.
My bedroom is my favourite room.
Write soon,
    Love,
        Ruth xx

1 Ruth lives in Nottingham.

false

2 Jameston is a small village.

....

3 Jameston hasn't got high buildings.

....

4 Ruth's house has got two floors.

....

5 There are four bedrooms in Ruth's house.

....

6 Ruth has got a brother and a sister.

....

7 Write a letter to a pen-friend

Describe your house and your favourite room.

8 Pairs game A

Speak and draw.

SWEETS

TOYS

SUPERMARKET

PARK

BOTTLES

Is there a book shop/flower shop/clothes shop/
pet shop/bus stop/paper bank in the picture?

Yes, there is. It's between/behind/in front of/next to …

Speak and draw.

FLOWERS

BOOKS

PETS

CLOTHES

PARK

BUS STOP

PAPER

CANS

*Is there a toy shop/sweet shop/supermarket/
telephone box/letter box/bottle bank in the picture?*

Yes, there is. It's between/behind/in front of/next to …

DO YOU KNOW THAT...?

Look at Pupil's Book page 44.

1 Crossword Find out and complete.

1 A Green organization.

2 A glass item.

3 The name of a plant.

4 A metal item.

5 The name of a sea.

6 The material people use to make newspapers.

7 A plastic item.

2 Read and tick (✓) True or false?

	True	False
1 The Mediterranean Sea is very polluted.	✓	
2 You can't swim in the Mediterranean Sea.		
3 The fumes from cars and buses are bad.		
4 Glass bottles can be recycled.		
5 Greenpeace is a green organization.		

7 KEEPING HEALTHY

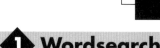 **Wordsearch** What's the matter? Find seven words

F	G	H	E	A	D	A	C	H	E
H	T	I	J	L	P	Q	R	S	A
A	U	O	C	O	L	D	C	T	R
W	M	K	O	K	T	U	V	X	A
B	M	F	U	T	C	E	G	R	C
I	Y	L	G	M	H	J	N	I	H
P	A	U	H	V	E	A	J	N	E
J	C	Q	A	N	S	I	C	G	R
P	H	R	S	L	U	R	D	H	A
A	E	B	F	I	J	L	A	U	E

....

....

....

....

....

....

....

2 What's the matter with them?

He's got a headache. ....

....

....

....

....

....

....

....

....

3 ▸ Number and read in order

☐ Little Red Hen makes the flour.

☐ Little Red Hen and her chicks eat the bread.

1 Little Red Hen finds some wheat.

☐ Little Red Hen makes the bread.

☐ Mr Dog, Mr Pig and Mr Duck have nothing.

☐ Little Red Hen cuts the wheat.

☐ Little Red Hen plants the wheat.

4 ▸ Listen and complete the chart

Who	When	Why
Mary	Monday	cough
Anna		
Tony		
Karen		
James		

flu

sore throat

cough

toothache

cold

5 Read, draw and write

1	2	3	4	5
Dog	plant		Woof! Woof!	toothache
Pig	cut		Oink! Oink!	tummyache
Duck	make		Quack! Quack!	a headache

Hello, Mr ...¹........... Can you help me to ...²........... this wheat?

⁴...................... Sorry, but I'm ill. I've got ⁵......................

Who can help me to ...²........... the wheat?

⁴...................... Sorry, I've got ⁵......................

Who can help me to ...²........... the flour?

⁴...................... Sorry, I've got ⁵......................

Who can help me to ...²........... the bread?

⁴...................... Sorry, I've got ⁵......................

Can I have some bread?

No, you can't! You're ill! This bread is for me and my chicks.

6 **Keeping healthy**   Circle the healthy habits. Write sentences.

Good habits

Drink milk.

....

....

....

Bad habits

Don't eat with dirty hands.

....

....

....

7 Find someone who ...

Maria eats lots of cakes.

.... doesn't play any sports.

.... watches lots of television.

.... goes to bed early.

.... brushes his/her teeth every morning.

.... comes to school on foot.

.... doesn't like fruit.

> Freddy, do you eat lots of cakes?
>
> No, I don't.
>
> Maria, do you eat lots of cakes?
>
> Yes, I do.

8 Write a healthy menu

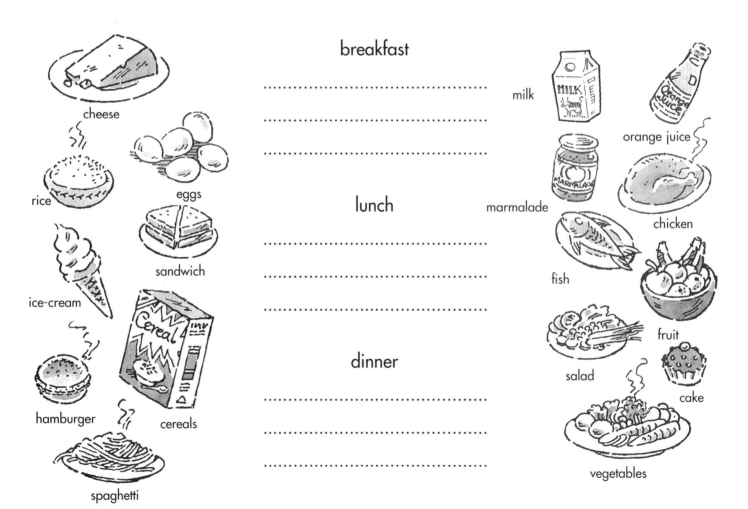

cheese

rice

eggs

ice-cream

sandwich

hamburger

cereals

spaghetti

milk

orange juice

marmalade

chicken

fish

salad

fruit

cake

vegetables

breakfast

....

....

....

lunch

....

....

....

dinner

....

....

....

DO YOU KNOW THAT...?

Look at Pupil's Book page 51.

1 Find and write

grass   bush   tree

Coffee beans are the fruit of a ....

Wheat is a type of ....

Tea comes from a ....

Cocoa beans are the fruit of a ....

2 Number and match

SUPER BUS STOP 4

 Test yourself How many words can you write?

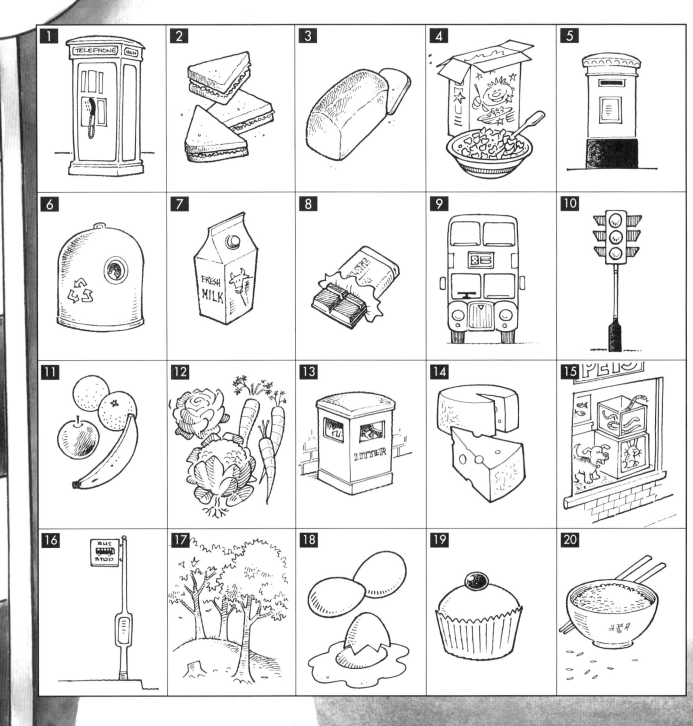

What is there in the street?

telephone box

....

....

....

What do you eat/drink?

meat

....

....

....

SCORE

1–6	Not very good. Study more.	14–17	Very good.
7–10	Okay, but you can do better.	18–20	Excellent. Well done!
11–13	Good.		

2 Write   What's the matter?

1 ....

....

2 ....

....

3 ....

....

4 ....

....

5 ....

....

6 ....

....

THANKSGIVING

1 **Solve and write**   *Pilgrim   Indian   pumpkin   turkey   corn*

1
2
3
4
5

☐ ....

☐ ....

☐ ....

☐ ....

1 *turkey* ....

2 **Read and circle the correct answer**

1 The Pilgrims …

   a come from England.

   b come from America.

   c come from Italy.

2 The Pilgrims …

   a go to England.

   b go to America.

   c go to Italy.

3 It's the year …

   a 1620.

   b 1920.

   c 2020.

4 The Pilgrims' plants …

   a grow very well.

   b don't grow.

   c are very tall.

5 The Pilgrims …

   a are happy.

   b are angry.

   c are hungry.

6 The Indians …

   a help the Pilgrims.

   b don't help the Pilgrims.

   c play with the Pilgrims.

❸ Match and write

1 The Pilgrims come

2 The Pilgrims go to

3 The plants

4 The Pilgrims are

5 The Indians

6 They say

very hungry.

help the Pilgrims.

America in the Mayflower.

'thank you' for the harvest.

do not grow.

from England.

1 *The Pilgrims came from England.*

2 ....

3 ....

4 ....

5 ....

6 ....

CHRISTMAS

1 Memory game Circle and match.

crackers   roast turkey   Christmas tree   Christmas cards   Christmas tree lights

star   holly   ivy   fruit   Christmas pudding

Christmas stocking   candle   mince pies   bells

2 Number and describe the pictures

a ☐

b ☐

g ☐

CHRISTMAS DINNER MENU

****

Roast turkey

Roast potatoes

Vegetables

****

Christmas pudding

****

Cheese and biscuits

****

Mince pies

****

Coffee

c ☐

f ☐

e ☐

d ☐

PANCAKE DAY

1 Match

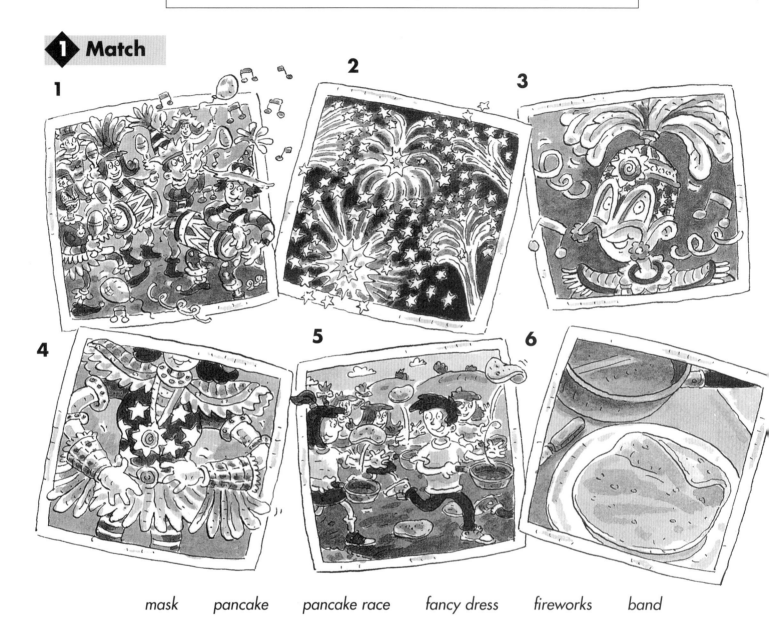

mask   pancake   pancake race   fancy dress   fireworks   band

2 Write

1 What day of the week is Pancake Day? ....

2 Is Pancake Day on the same date each year? ....

3 What date is Pancake Day this year? ....

4 What do you call Pancake Day? ....

5 Do you eat anything special on this day? ....

6 Do you wear masks and fancy dress? ....

3 Read and number

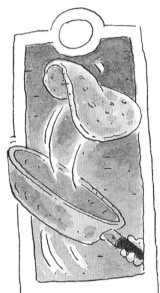

Toss the pancake and cook the other side.

Put some sugar and lemon on the pancake and eat it.

Stir the mixture and add a glass of milk.

1

Mix some flour, salt and an egg in a bowl.

Put some mixture in a frying pan and cook one side of the pancake.

4 Draw and write

What do you need to make a pancake?

Pancake recipe
I need:
....
....
....
....
....
....

GULLIVER IN LILLIPUT

1 Match

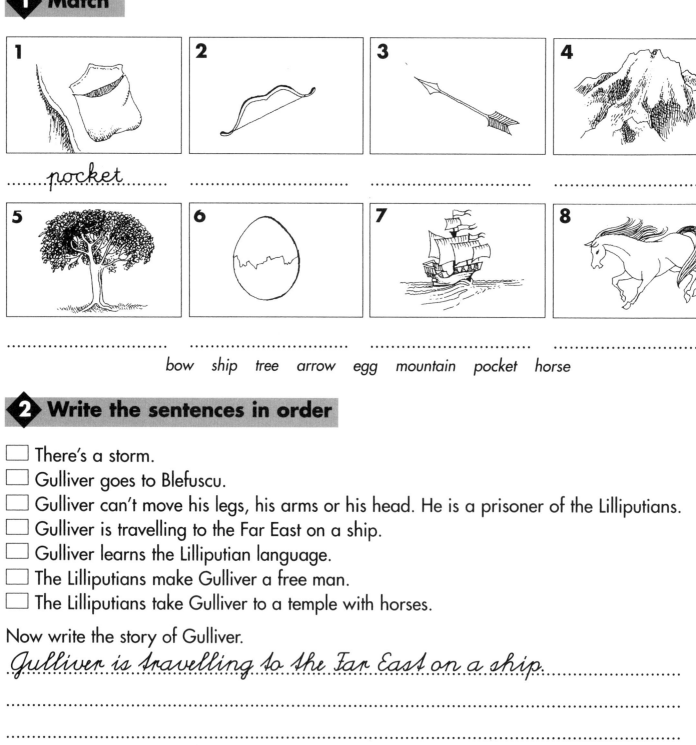

1 ....pocket....

2 ....

3 ....

4 ....

5 ....

6 ....

7 ....

8 ....

bow   ship   tree   arrow   egg   mountain   pocket   horse

2 Write the sentences in order

☐ There's a storm.
☐ Gulliver goes to Blefuscu.
☐ Gulliver can't move his legs, his arms or his head. He is a prisoner of the Lilliputians.
☐ Gulliver is travelling to the Far East on a ship.
☐ Gulliver learns the Lilliputian language.
☐ The Lilliputians make Gulliver a free man.
☐ The Lilliputians take Gulliver to a temple with horses.

Now write the story of Gulliver.

Gulliver is travelling to the Far East on a ship.

....

....

....

....

....

She's
reading

They're
dancing

He's
laughing

It's
running

They're
playing

It's
running

They're
dancing

She's
reading

It's
running

She's
reading

He's
writing

They're
dancing

He's
writing

He's
laughing

She's
swimming

He's
writing

He's
writing

They're
dancing

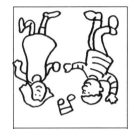

It's
running

They're
playing

He's
laughing

She's
swimming

They're
dancing

He's
writing

It's
running

She's
swimming

She's
swimming

It's
running

Cut out **3** Board Game ✂

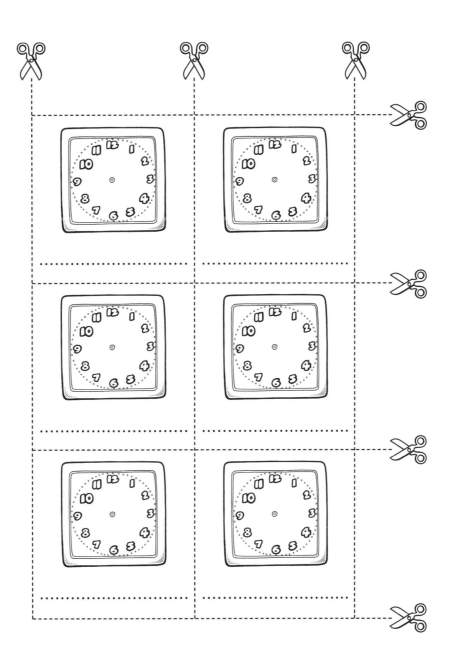

Cut out **4** The weather

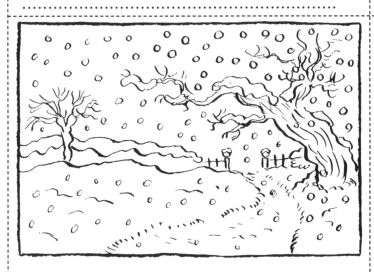

Thanksgiving Book

Date ....

To ....

....

....

From ....

Macmillan Education
4 Crinan Street
London N1 9XW
A division of Macmillan Publishers Limited
Companies and representatives throughout the world

ISBN 978-1-4050-7693-7

Text © María José Lobo   Pepita Subirà 2005
Design and illustration © Macmillan Publishers
Limited 2005

First published 2005

Designed by Cox Design Partnership, Witney, Oxon

Cover illustration by Geo Parkin

Illustrated by: David Lock, Matthew Doyle, Tony De
Saulles, Karen Donnelly, John Haslam, Susan Hellard,
Ann Johns, Derek Matthews, Kevin McAleenan, Geo
Parkin and Kathy Baxendale.

Printed and bound in China

2018 2017 2016
19 18 17 16 15